1751

800
AB
FRE

THIS WALKER BOOK BELONGS TO:

COMMA CATERPILLARS

ORANGE TIP CATERPILLARS

PEACOCK CATERPILLARS

It's impossible to say exactly when
you'll find caterpillars. It depends on where
you live, and what the weather's like, and all sorts
of other things. The eggs I found were laid in May.
They hatched out into caterpillars in June and changed
their skins four times during the next month or so. The first
three times I didn't see it happen, because they changed
inside their tents. But I did see the fourth time…
The caterpillar on the pea sticks pupated
in the middle of July and became
a butterfly in August.

For my grandfather, S.H.K., with love
V.F.
For Robert and Chloe
C.V.

First published 1993 by
Walker Books Ltd, 87 Vauxhall Walk
London SE11 5HJ

This edition published 1995

2 4 6 8 10 9 7 5 3 1

Text © 1993 Vivian French
Illustrations © 1993 Charlotte Voake

This book has been typeset in
Calligraphic 810

Printed in Hong Kong

British Library Cataloguing in Publication Data
A catalogue record for this book is available from the
British Library.

ISBN 0-7445-3636-7

CATERPILLAR CATERPILLAR

WRITTEN BY
Vivian French

ILLUSTRATED BY
Charlotte Voake

WALKER BOOKS
AND SUBSIDIARIES
LONDON • BOSTON • SYDNEY

My father and my grandfather both liked gardening very much, but my grandfather used to grow stinging nettles. My father didn't; he said they were weeds, and rooted them out.

"Why don't you get rid of your nettles?" I asked my grandfather.

"Stinging nettles grow butterflies," he said. "Go and look."

I went and looked. I couldn't see any butterflies, though. My grandfather turned one of the nettle leaves over to show me the bumps on the back of it, but I didn't know what they were.

"Butterfly eggs," said my grandfather.

"What sort of butterflies?"

My grandfather peered closely at the bumps.
"Haven't got my specs on," he said, "but they could
be Tortoiseshells, or Peacocks. They both like nettles.
If you keep an eye on them you'll see when
the caterpillars hatch out."

"Won't they crawl away?" I asked.

My grandfather straightened up
and looked down at me.

"Humph," he said.

"You just keep watching."

So I did.

NETTLES WILL
STING YOU IF YOU
TOUCH THEM,
BUT THEY
WON'T STING
THE CATERPILLARS.

THE EGGS ARE DOME-SHAPED, WITH LITTLE RIDGES. EACH EGG IS ABOUT THE SIZE OF THE TOP OF A PIN.

MOST BUTTERFLIES LAY THEIR EGGS IN ONES AND TWOS, MOVING FROM PLANT TO PLANT. PEACOCK AND TORTOISESHELL BUTTERFLIES LAY LOTS OF EGGS AT ONCE.

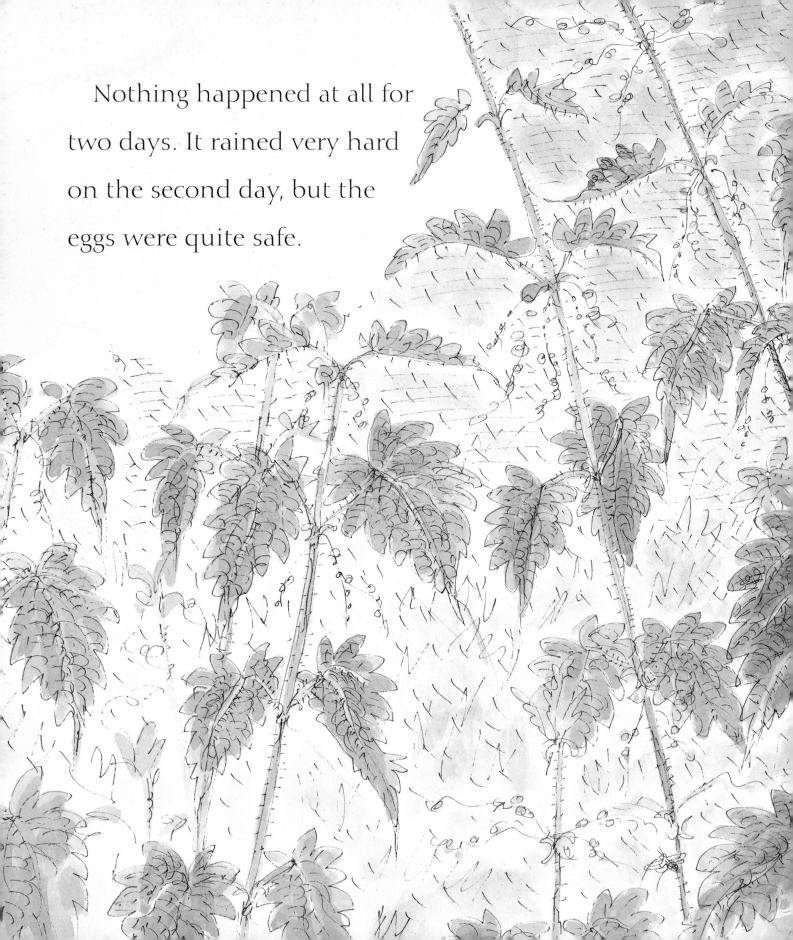

Nothing happened at all for two days. It rained very hard on the second day, but the eggs were quite safe.

The next day there were lots and lots
of little tiny caterpillars crawling on the
nettle leaves. The eggs were papery
and empty. I squashed some
with my fingernail.

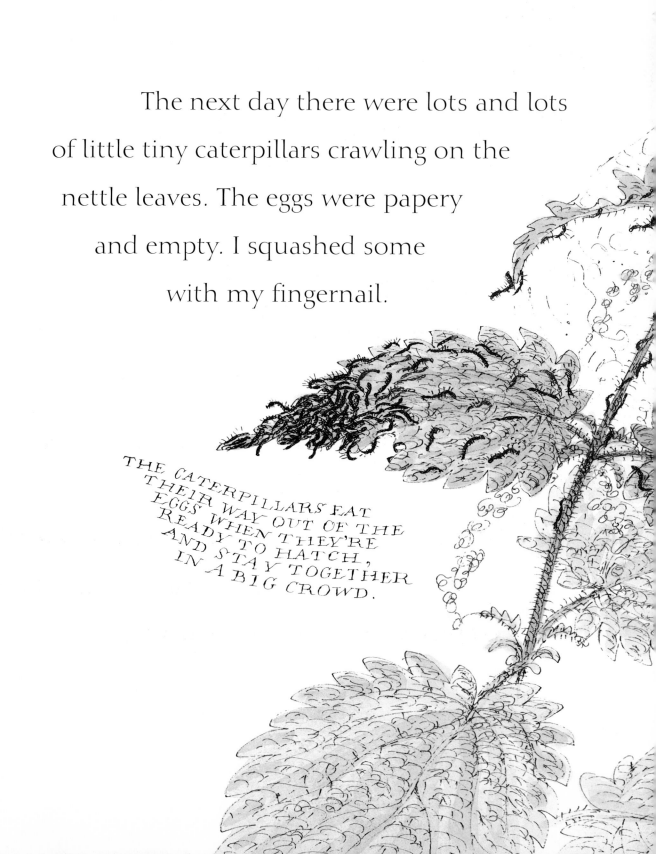

THE CATERPILLARS EAT
THEIR WAY OUT OF THE
EGGS WHEN THEY'RE
READY TO HATCH,
AND STAY TOGETHER
IN A BIG CROWD.

THEY MAKE A WEB OF
WHITE SILK BETWEEN
THE STEM OF THE PLANT
AND THE LEAVES.
IT'S LIKE A TENT.

WHEN THEY'VE EATEN
ALL THE LEAVES NEARBY,
THEY MOVE ON AND
MAKE A NEW TENT.

My grandfather came over to see

what I was doing.

"Ah," he said, "Peacock caterpillars."

"Do they eat cabbage?" I asked.

I'd seen caterpillars on cabbages.

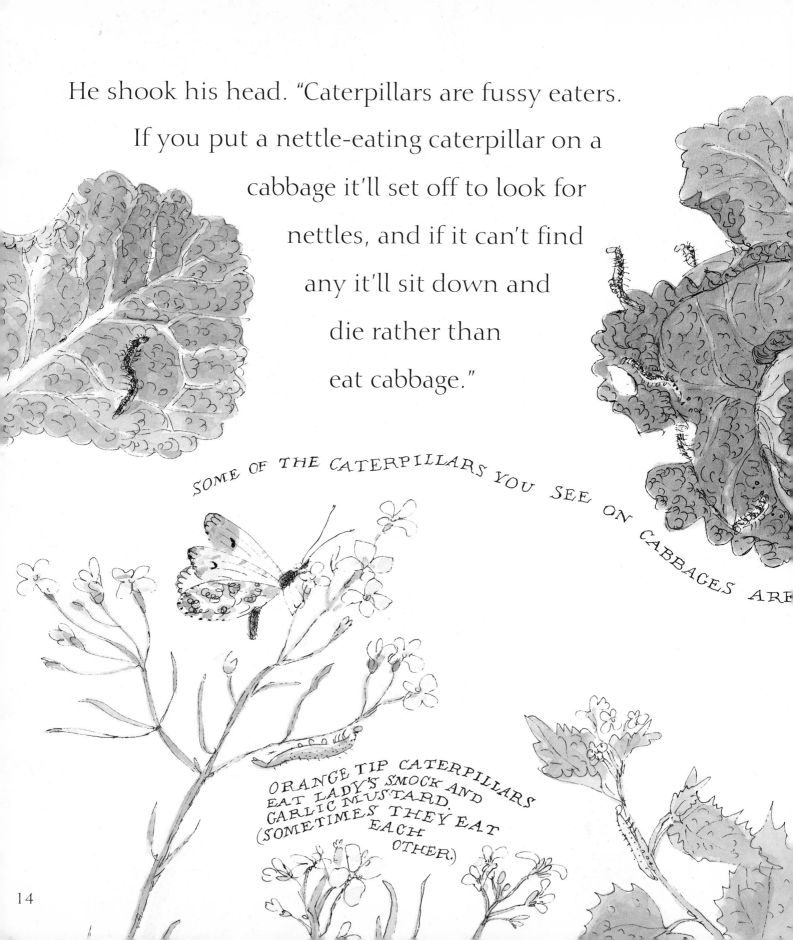

He shook his head. "Caterpillars are fussy eaters. If you put a nettle-eating caterpillar on a cabbage it'll set off to look for nettles, and if it can't find any it'll sit down and die rather than eat cabbage."

SOME OF THE CATERPILLARS YOU SEE ON CABBAGES ARE

ORANGE TIP CATERPILLARS EAT LADY'S SMOCK AND GARLIC MUSTARD. (SOMETIMES THEY EAT EACH OTHER.)

COMMA CATERPILLARS LIKE HOPS BEST, BUT SOMETIMES THEY HAVE TO MAKE DO WITH NETTLES.

CABBAGE WHITES. THEY LOVE CABBAGE.

PEACOCK, SMALL TORTOISESHELL AND RED ADMIRAL CATERPILLARS ALL LIKE NETTLES BEST.

THE CATERPILLARS LEAVE LITTLE DROPPINGS WHEREVER THEY GO.

AS THEY GET BIGGER, YOU CAN SEE THEIR WHITE SPOTS MORE CLEARLY.

THEY DON'T MIND WHICH WAY UP THEY EAT, AND THEY HARDLY EVER STOP EATING.

I looked at my Peacock caterpillars.

They were all together in a little

crowd, eating as fast as they could.

"Won't the birds eat them?" I asked.

"Couldn't we cover them up?"

"No need," said my grandfather.

"Caterpillars that don't hide away are really saying,

'I'm poisonous – keep off!' And the birds know that."

He pulled his pipe out of his pocket and very,
very gently nudged one of the caterpillars.

It curled itself up at once and fell off the leaf.

"There," he said. "Even if something does come along
looking for a snack, the caterpillar might still escape."

"Can I make one curl up?" I stuck my finger out.

"Don't touch them," my grandfather said.

"Some spiny caterpillars can give you a rash,
and other kinds leave a nasty smell on
your fingers. Besides, you might hurt them."

THEY HAVE VELVETY BODIES AND SHINY HEADS.
LOOK AT THEIR SPINY BACKS!
THEY HAVE THREE PAIRS OF LEGS
AT THE FRONT, WITH LITTLE
CLAWS ON THEM, AND
STUMPIER LEGS
FURTHER DOWN.

I went on watching the caterpillars.

They were getting bigger. By the second Saturday in July they had eaten nearly all the plant they had hatched out on and were crawling over the other nettles.

Some of them were lying completely still, though, and not eating at all. All of a sudden one of them gave a little wriggle and its skin split right open. Inside was another brand new caterpillar, and it crawled out of the old skin as if it were crawling out of a sleeping-bag. It looked quite fresh and clean, and it seemed to be bigger than before. All the other caterpillars changed skins too.

WHEN IT'S READY TO CHANGE ITS SKIN, A CATERPILLAR SPINS A LITTLE SILK MAT ON THE LEAF AND FASTENS ITS LAST TWO LEGS TO IT.

I knew something must be eating my caterpillars, because by now there weren't so many of them.

I didn't mind that, but I did mind five days later when I found that every single one of them had disappeared.

"Where have they gone?" I asked. I was close to tears. "Pea sticks," said my grandfather. We marched round the corner of the shed to where the pea sticks were. "Sometimes one or two come here," my grandfather said.

"Ah, yes, here we are." Sure enough,
there was one of the caterpillars,
hanging head downwards off a pea stick.
And to my amazement, before my very
eyes, its skin began to peel off from
its head upwards ... and shrivelled away.

This time there wasn't another
caterpillar ready to come out.
Instead there was something
like a little soft brown bag, hanging
on the pea stick. It didn't have legs or eyes or
anything, and it dried up into a little case.

My grandfather said that was just what it was,

but the proper name for it was a pupa.

"But where's the caterpillar gone?" I asked.

All the bits of caterpillar were inside the case,

he said, and they were changing.

WHEN THEY'RE READY TO
PUPATE, THE
CATERPILLARS
LEAVE THEIR
NETTLES.

EACH ONE OF THEM
FINDS A
PLACE TO
BE ON ITS
OWN.

IT MIGHT BE UP A
TREE, A FENCE,
A STICK, OR A TWIG.

EACH
CATERPILLAR
MAKES
A TINY WHITE
PAD...

THEN
ATTACHES ITS
BACK LEGS TO
IT, AND HANGS
UPSIDE DOWN.

SOON ITS SKIN PEELS
OFF, LEAVING BEHIND
A BEAUTIFUL PUPA.
IT'S GREEN IF IT'S ON
A LEAF, AND BROWN
IF IT'S ON A
TWIG.

Just this once, I was allowed to bring the stick with the little case on it into the kitchen. I watched for ten whole days and on the tenth day the pupa went very, very dark.

The next morning I was eating my breakfast when my grandfather suddenly said, "LOOK!"

I rushed to see, and the case of the pupa

had split. Something was crawling out ...

but it didn't look a bit like a butterfly.

It was crumpled, and it looked damp,

and it wasn't at all a pretty colour.

"It must have gone wrong,"
I said, feeling very sad.

Very gently, my grandfather

lifted the stick and put it on

the window-ledge in the sunshine.

The creature crawled slowly up

the stick, and stopped.

Little by little it began to stretch out.

It was just like watching a flower

unfolding itself, only it had

wings instead of petals.

THE WINGS
OF THE
BUTTERFLY
UNFOLD AS LIQUID
IS PUMPED INTO
ITS VEINS.
THE WINGS HAVE
TO DRY FOR AN
HOUR OR TWO
BEFORE IT
CAN FLY

And the wings began to tremble, and to shine in the sunlight, and then suddenly there it was – a real butterfly, with spidery legs and its wings spread wide open.

It was so lovely that I couldn't say anything at all. Then its wings fluttered and it flew off into the garden – the very newest butterfly there.

COMMA

PEACOCK

RED ADMIRAL

Index

COMMA

Look up the pages to find out about
all these caterpillar and butterfly things.
Don't forget to look at both kinds of words:
this kind and THIS KIND.

LARGE WHITE

ORANGE TIP

ORANGE TIP

COMMON BLUE

COMMON BLUE
CATERPILLAR

MORE WALKER PAPERBACKS
For You to Enjoy

"These books fulfil all the requirements of a factual picture book, but also supply that imaginative element." *The Independent on Sunday*

"Beautifully illustrated books, written with style and humour." *The Times Educational Supplement*

ALL PIGS ARE BEAUTIFUL
by Dick-King Smith/Anita Jeram
0-7445-3635-9

CATERPILLAR CATERPILLAR
by Vivian French/Charlotte Voake
0-7445-3636-7

THINK OF A BEAVER
by Karen Wallace/Mick Manning
0-7445-3638-3

THINK OF AN EEL
by Karen Wallace/Mike Bostock
(Winner of the Times Educational Supplement Junior Information
Book Award and the Kurt Maschler Award)
0-7445-3639-1

WHAT IS A WALL, AFTER ALL?
by Judy Allen/Alan Baron
0-7445-3640-5

I LIKE MONKEYS BECAUSE…
by Peter Hansard/Patricia Casey
0-7445-3646-4

A FIELD FULL OF HORSES
by Peter Hansard/Kenneth Lilly
0-7445-3645-6

A PIECE OF STRING IS A WONDERFUL THING
by Judy Hindley/Margaret Chamberlain
0-7445-3637-5

£4.99 each